Inventions That CHANGED the WORLD

How Electricity Changed the World

Bethany Bryan

Cavendish Square
New York

Published in 2019 by Cavendish Square Publishing, LLC
243 5th Avenue, Suite 136, New York, NY 10016

First Edition

Library of Congress Cataloging-in-Publication Data

Names: Bryan, Bethany, author.
Title: How electricity changed the world / Bethany Bryan.
Description: First edition. | New York : Cavendish Square, 2019. |
Series: Inventions that changed the world | Includes bibliographical references and index. | Audience: Age 10-13. | Audience: Grade 5 to 8.
Identifiers: LCCN 2018024820 (print) | LCCN 2018026374 (ebook) | ISBN 9781502641069 (ebook) | ISBN 9781502641052 (library bound) | ISBN 9781502641045 (pbk.)
Subjects: LCSH: Electrical engineering--History--Juvenile literature | Electrical engineering--Social aspects--Juvenile literature | Power resources--Juvenile literature.
Classification: LCC TK148 (ebook) | LCC TK148 .B788 2019 (print) | DDC 303.48/3--dc23
LC record available at https://lccn.loc.gov/2018024820

Editorial Director: David McNamara
Editor: Kristen Susienka
Copy Editor: Alex Tessman
Associate Art Director: Alan Sliwinski
Designer: Joe Parenteau
Production Coordinator: Karol Szymczuk
Photo Research: J8 Media

The photographs in this book are used by permission and through the courtesy of: Cover, p. 1; NASA Earth Observatory/Wikimedia Commons/File:Nile River Delta at Night.jpg/CC PD; p. 4 imaginima/E+/Getty Images; p. 6 Charles Wayne Lytton/Shutterstock.com; p. 7 Jeff Greenberg/Universal Images Group/Getty Images; p. 9 Arthur Rothstein/Library of Congress; p. 10, 39 Science & Society Picture Library/Getty Images; p. 12 Neil Lockhart/Shutterstock.com; p. 14 Ironie/Wikimedia Commons/File:Ironie pile Bagdad.jpg/CC BY-SA 2.5; p. 16 Look and Learn/Bridgeman Images; p. 18 Hulton Archive/Getty Images; p. 20 Underwood Archives/Archive Photos/Getty Images; p. 23, 37 Bettmann/Getty Images; p. 28 Andy Nelson/The Christian Science Monitor/Getty Images; p. 31 cozyta/Shutterstock.com; p. 33 Hulton Archive/Getty Images; p. 40 Milena Moiola/Shutterstock.com; p. 43 Lukasz Z/Shutterstock.com; p. 44 deebrowning/iStock; p. 48 Oyvind Gravas/Woldcam/Cover Images/Newscom; p. 49 jhorrocks/iStock; p. 52 Patrick T. Fallon/Bloomberg/Getty Images; p. 53 Yoshikazu Tsuno/AFP/Getty Images; p. 54 David Paul Morris/Bloomberg/Getty Images.

Printed in the United States of America

CONTENTS

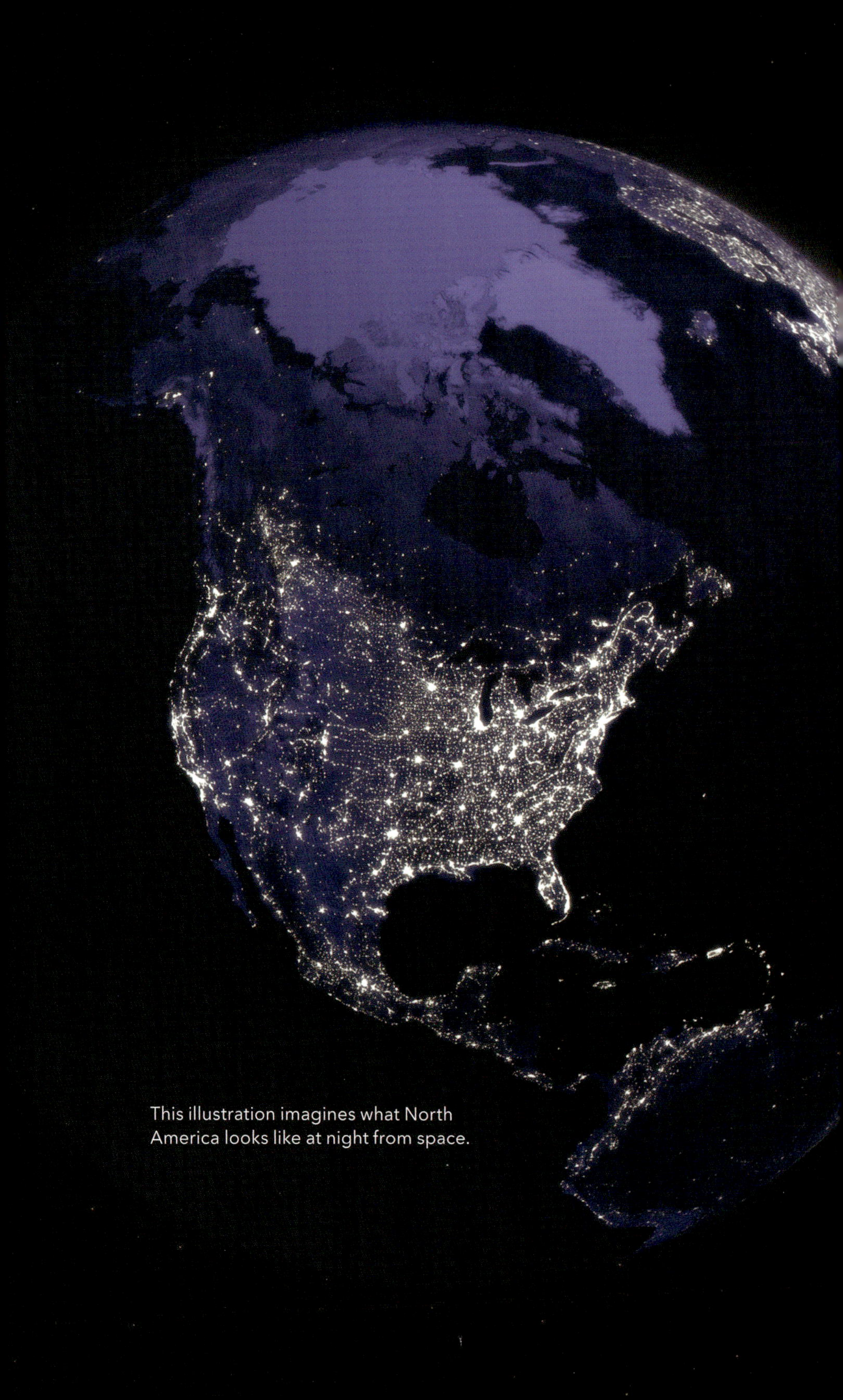

This illustration imagines what North America looks like at night from space.

CHAPTER

ONE

A World Without Power

Many might find it difficult to imagine a world without electricity. Humans rely on electricity and all of the appliances and technology it powers so much that most people barely think about it, unless there's a blackout during a storm or a blown fuse on a dark night. During these times, people know that soon life as normal will resume. The lights will come back on, and the Netflix marathon can continue. But what if electricity, in the form we know it today, didn't exist at all? For thousands of years, it didn't. Electricity existed in nature—in the form of a spark when two pieces of fabric rubbed together, lightning storms, and even in the human body. However, for a very long time, humans didn't know how to use electricity for power. It was mysterious, even frightening for some. So they relied on other sources of light, heat, and power to do many things humans can do today with the flick of a switch, the click of a mouse, or the press of a button.

Life Before Electricity

Before electricity, the main source of heat and light was fire. People lit their homes with lanterns, candles, and gas lamps. Heat for cooking and warmth also came from fire. Fire came from burning wood, kerosene, coal, and other sources of fuel, depending on what was available and inexpensive. In areas where there weren't a lot of trees, and kerosene and coal weren't readily available, people burned dried cow manure.

Finding the fuel to build and maintain a single fire is time-consuming, but before electricity, people weren't just responsible for a single fire for a few hours, like we might enjoy a campfire today. They were responsible for heating their homes for an entire day, an entire week, an entire winter. To do this, people spent a lot of time chopping wood and storing coal and other fuels.

Gas lighting used in homes grew in popularity in the early 1800s. Today, most homes use electricity for lighting.

Food was also a more time-consuming process

before electricity. Without electric refrigeration, people had to find ways to preserve fruits and vegetables for the lean winter months by salting, canning, drying, or freezing them. The process was similar with meat, fish, and other proteins. Those who lived in rural areas, away from food markets, often butchered or hunted their own animals and grew their own crops and vegetables, and then tried to preserve them.

Water was also more labor-intensive before electricity. Today, water is delivered into homes via pumps that run

A trip to the Homestead and Living History Museum in Gainesville, Florida, offers visitors the chance to pump water from a well the same way people did in the centuries before they had access to electricity.

DID YOU KNOW:

Life was much dirtier before electricity. In 1900, health officials in Rochester, New York, calculated that the city's fifteen thousand horses produced enough poop to create a pile 175 feet (53 meters) high and covering 1 acre (0.4 hectare) of land.

on electricity. Before this technology was available, water was hand-pumped from the ground or collected from streams. According to a study by the US Department of Agriculture in 1919, families in rural areas spent ten hours every week just hauling water. This water was used for baths, cooking, and washing clothes by hand.

While people still rely on horses, cattle, and other working animals for certain tasks today, before electricity sparked mass production of cars, trucks, and tractors, animals were the main mode of transportation and source of farm labor. On horseback, traveling to a town 50 miles (80 kilometers) away might take a few days. An oxen and plow covered significantly less ground in a day than modern farming equipment. Working animals also required food, water, land to graze, and a clean, safe shelter.

The Electricity Revolution

The year 1882 marked the beginning of the electricity revolution in the United States, with the founding of the Edison Electric Illuminating Company of New

York. For the first time, useable electricity arrived in homes—although this was limited to parts of the city of Manhattan at first. By 1925, half of the homes in America had electricity, most of which were in urban

Working for the Rural Electrification Administration often required linemen like the one shown here, high up on a pole in Hayti, Missouri, to be unafraid of heights.

THE TELEGRAPH

Cooke and Wheatstone's five-needle telegraph system was only in use for about a year before the wire insulation broke down and left it unable to be operated.

Before the electric telegraph, people used a variety of methods to communicate across long distances. Drums, smoke signals, and semaphore, or sending messages by flag, were some of the early ways that people did so, but these were affected by the weather and other conditions. The invention of the telegraph changed everything.

In the 1830s, British inventors William Cooke and Charles Wheatstone created a device with five needles that could be pointed at letters and numbers using electricity to create messages, but the technology was slow and rudimentary. It was around this same time that Samuel Morse was developing a telegraph of his own while also creating a code that would help send messages more efficiently. This code would become known as the Morse code.

The telegraph would soon be overshadowed by the telephone and fall into disuse not even a century after its invention. However, it remains the first form of instantaneous electric long-distance communication.

areas. Rural areas soon followed with the founding of the Rural Electrification Administration (REA) in 1935. Building power lines across the country was an expensive endeavor, and companies were not interested in taking on that expense. The REA was created by the Roosevelt administration to encourage farmers to create electricity cooperatives, where a group of citizens invests in and raises funds for a mutual benefit—in this case electricity. When Franklin Delano Roosevelt passed away in 1945, 90 percent of farms had electricity because of cooperatives.

The arrival of electricity completely revolutionized how people lived, especially in these rural areas. Electricity freed up a lot of hours in the day that people previously used for gathering firewood, washing clothes by hand, and preserving and stockpiling food. The first Industrial Revolution was already under way in the late 1800s because of the invention of steam engines. Their use in factories forever changed the way that items were built. However, when electricity arrived, it ushered in a second Industrial Revolution, one that gave factories safer, more efficient ways of producing products, changed the way that people traveled and transported materials, and lured more people to cities. Today, electricity plays a part in almost every moment of many people's daily lives. It is used in the manufacture of almost everything we touch. It has become essential to modern existence.

Early scientists were fascinated with and studied lightning.

CHAPTER TWO

Harnessing the Power

Electricity isn't an "invention" in the way the steam engine, the internet, the printing press, or the telephone are. It has existed naturally throughout time. It is, simply, a flow of electrons, and electrons exist in every atom. People who have been credited with "inventing" electricity—Benjamin Franklin, Thomas Edison, and Nikola Tesla, for instance—invented the means for harnessing, or using, the power of electricity. They studied it and learned how to master it, building off of ideas from previous generations of inventors, scientists, and scholars.

Today, humans have access to electric power because of thousands of years of work done by countless individuals. Some of these people rose to fame on their discoveries, and others' names have been lost to time.

Early Evidence of Electricity

No one can really say where the earliest experiments using electricity took place. However, there is evidence that around 600 BCE, the ancient Greeks discovered that after rubbing fossilized pine sap, or amber, against animal fur, small pieces of straw or grass would stick to the fossil when held near them. This discovery is now called static electricity.

In 1938, according to legend, a German archaeologist named Wilhelm Konig was excavating a site just outside of Baghdad, Iraq, when he unearthed a clay jar about 5 inches (13 centimeters) long. Inside the jar was a copper cylinder that contained an iron rod, and there was evidence that the jar had once contained an acidic substance like vinegar or wine. Konig decided that the jar, which dated back to around 200 BCE, had likely once been a type of battery. Several more of these "batteries" were unearthed. Then World War II broke out, and the discovery was temporarily forgotten.

People have since made replicas of the Baghdad batteries, as they have come to be known, and they can conduct a few volts of electricity. But no one can say for certain what they were actually used for. Some think that the batteries may have been used to help ease pain by using a small electrical

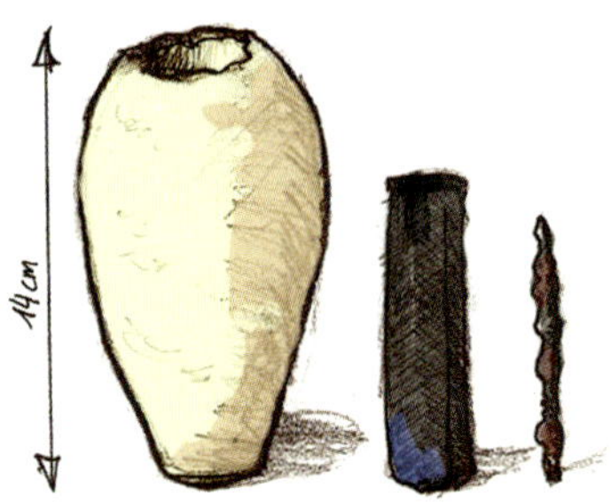

Baghdad batteries consist of three parts: a ceramic pot, a copper tube, and an iron rod, as this image illustrates.

current to stimulate nerve endings. Others suspect the jar was used for electroplating, or transferring a thin coat of one metal onto another metal surface using electricity. No matter its purpose, it shows signs that electricity had some use as far back as ancient Mesopotamia.

First Experiments

Static electricity was known as the "amber effect" in the sixteenth century. That is because its early experiments involved amber. This was the case when Sir William Gilbert studied magnetism and what he came to call "electric attraction." He conducted experiments using magnetic iron ore. He wanted to better understand the magnetic pull of Earth's core. Historians often credit Gilbert with being the first scientist to distinguish between magnetic and electrical attraction. In 1663, Otto von Guircke invented a machine that created static electricity by applying friction to a ball of sulfur. By 1729, scientist Stephen Gray had begun to study how electricity was conducted. He was one of the first people to do so. Gray rubbed a glass tube to charge it and then watched as sparks seemed to leap from the tube to the things that surrounded it. Further, and more popular, stories of conducting electricity would come in the decades following.

Benjamin Franklin's Key Experiment

There are a lot of misconceptions about Benjamin Franklin's experiments with electricity. One is that Franklin *discovered* electricity. However, scientists had been studying the phenomenon for centuries by the time

Benjamin Franklin's kite experiment has gone down in history as one of the great moments in science, but some historians speculate on whether it really happened.

a lightning storm arrived on a June afternoon in 1752. Franklin's plan was simply to prove a hypothesis that he had outlined in a letter to his friend, fellow scientist Peter Collinson, in 1750. Franklin had an idea that a piece of metal held high in the air could gather an electric charge during a lightning storm. This charge could be sent to and stored in a Leyden jar. The Leyden jar was made for this very purpose. His findings would help him perfect an invention that would become the lightning rod.

Franklin made a kite and attached some wire to the top of it. To fly the kite, he used a long piece of hemp string, which would get wet in the rain and better conduct electricity. To that, he attached a house key, and to that, a long piece of silk string. The silk string, and Franklin, who held it, would remain dry, safe in the doorway of a nearby shed.

As the storm continued to build, so did the ambient energy in the air around the kite. The ambient energy created an electrical charge. It traveled down the string and into the metal key, where it would be stored temporarily, as Franklin predicted.

As it turns out, lightning didn't actually strike the kite. If it had, Franklin would likely have been killed. In fact, a Russian scientist named Georg Wilhelm Reichmann conducted a similar experiment a year later and was struck by a bolt of lightning. He died instantly.

Galvani and Volta

At the start of the nineteenth century, it was believed that there were two types of electricity: natural electricity (lightning) and artificial electricity (static). Biologist Luigi Galvani believed that he had discovered a third type, one created within animal tissue. Galvani had long been performing experiments using dead frogs. Sometimes, a frog's legs seemed to twitch when they came in contact with different kinds of metals.

Alessandro Volta disagreed with Galvani, his longtime rival. Volta believed that the electric current came not from the frog's tissue, but from the metals used in the experiment coming in contact with the damp flesh. To prove his theory, Volta also began to experiment using metals and frogs' legs. In 1800, his research led to the invention of a device that produced an electrical current, using saltwater-soaked cloths layered with copper and zinc discs. This invention was called a voltaic pile. It was one of the first modern batteries.

The voltaic pile brought Volta incredible acclaim. The French emperor Napoleon was so impressed by the invention that he made Volta a count.

The voltaic pile was the only invention of its kind at the time. It would be used as a reliable source of power

This Indonesian family makes do with a kerosene lamp after a tsunami destroyed their home in 2004.

CHAPTER THREE

Electricity's Impact

Electricity is available on every continent today, powering the majority of Earth's population. According to a 2015 article in the *Washington Post*, 1.3 billion people live without electricity. Often this is because of damage to buildings and power facilities during times of war or lack of development due to poverty, especially in rural regions. Building and maintaining machinery that provides electrical power to a nation is costly. Producing electricity requires a lot of resources, such as fuel and the equipment needed to turn it into energy.

How Electricity Is Made

Electricity is produced by power plants. There are over eight thousand power plants operating in the United States today. Every power plant contains a generator that produces electricity. It does this through the help of a fuel source. The type or types of fuel the generator uses varies. This is determined by location and availability of local fuel sources. Examples are coal, natural gas, and petroleum. These items are often referred to as "fossil fuels" since they come from the remains of once-living organisms.

Fossil fuels can be mined in the United States, but in some regions, it's actually more cost-effective to get fuel from other countries. Therefore, US fuel resources are made up of a combination of imports and mining or drilling on American soil. Where imports come from is determined by the price of the item and the cost of shipping it. The cost of these fossil fuels, however, along with reliance on foreign resources and the side effects of burning these types of fuels, has led to discovering other ways to provide power for Americans and the rest of the world.

As of 2017, nuclear power provides 20 percent of electricity in the United States. This power comes from over sixty nuclear power plants across the nation. Energy is created inside a nuclear reactor by splitting uranium atoms. This is called fission. The heat from this process is used to power steam turbines.

Other sources of energy include biomass, hydropower, wind energy, solar power, and geothermal power. Biomass comes from the burning of biological residue. Examples of biomass include scrap lumber, manure, forest debris, and certain crops. Energy from biomass fuels makes up about 4 percent of the total energy consumed in the United States. Solar energy and geothermal energy are also valuable sources of power in the United States. Together they make up 2 percent of the total energy consumed in the country.

Powering Homes

After power is produced by a generator, it has to travel long distances to get to where it's needed, so it is sent through a transformer. The transformer increases the voltage of the alternating current. There are special lines for transporting power at this level. They are called transmission lines. They are held up by a series of tall metal towers. These transmission lines take the power quickly to substations. There, the voltage is lowered so that is can cross power lines. Before electricity enters a home, it travels through another transformer. This one decreases the power. Wires then carry this electricity into homes. A meter monitors the amount of power being used in the home. Customers pay for the amount of energy used according to the meter.

Power plants are usually built outside of cities because they require a large area of land and often a water source, like a river, to work.

The Impact of Electricity

Having electricity at our fingertips is a marvel of science. It has given humans countless inventions and innovations that have changed their lives for the better. But what is the total impact of electricity? In the century and a half since electricity left the lab and entered everyday lives, scientists have discovered that not all of its impact has been positive. Burning fossil fuels has been proven to damage the environment. People have become dependent on electricity to where there are concerns that if and when these resources run out, it could lead to global and economic collapse.

If you take a look around at the objects surrounding you, it may be difficult to find something that hasn't been touched by electricity in some way. Even nonelectrical items were probably made by machines that run on electricity. Electricity has changed many industries, making possible ideas that once seemed only fantasy.

Electrical Appliances

In the twentieth century, the rise of household appliances helped people look after their living spaces in an easier and faster way. Many historians argue that inventions like the dishwasher, the vacuum cleaner, and the washing machine had the most impact on society. Each item gave women—who had traditionally been responsible for household upkeep, cooking, and cleaning—more time to pursue their personal interests. They even allowed many women to get a job outside of the home.

Washing clothes for an entire family once involved filling a washtub with soapy water and washing one piece of clothing at a time. Many people used a washboard to scrub their clothes. Then in 1908, Alva Fisher introduced the first electric-powered washing machine. It could wash a load of laundry at once. In the 1930s, an inventor named John W. Chamberlain improved upon existing electric washing machines by introducing one that could not only wash but also rinse and wring water from clothes. Other advances in clothing care came later. The first electric clothes dryer was introduced in 1915. Electric irons were introduced in 1903, and by 1927, they came with a temperature control that could be adjusted to the user's preference.

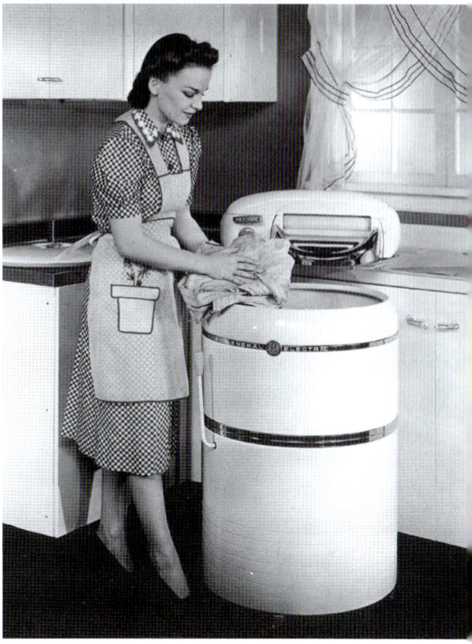

This 1947 photograph shows a woman using a General Electric washing machine. The contraption at the top is used to wring water from the clothing.

There have also been life-changing developments in appliances used for cleaning. The first vacuum for the home was introduced in 1907. James Spangler created a rudimentary device using an electric fan for suction, a filter made from a pillowcase, and a broomstick handle. Unsuccessful in developing and marketing the device himself, he sold his invention to a relative named William Hoover, who launched the Hoover Company. You can still

DAYLIGHT SAVING TIME

Every spring, many countries around the world take part in daylight saving time. This is when the clocks go forward by one hour. Daylight saving time was first proposed in the early twentieth century. It was a way to lower costs of lighting homes during hours of darkness. On March 19, 1918, during World War I, this plan first went into effect in the United States. It was believed that people who got off work when it was still light outside were far more likely to go shopping. This would ultimately help the economy. Although many think daylight saving time was meant to help farmers, they were actually against the plan because it gave them less time in the morning than before.

Today, whether or not daylight saving time actually helps save on energy costs is questionable. According to a 2008 study on the residents of Indiana, moving the clocks ahead actually increased energy use by 1 percent. Researchers concluded that while the cost of electricity used to light homes went down, costs for heating and cooling homes went up.

purchase a Hoover vacuum today. The first dishwasher went on the market in 1913, making the process of washing dishes much easier and less time consuming.

Improving cooking methods was one of the most important ways that electricity changed lives at home. The electric toaster, the automatic coffeemaker, and the microwave all made cooking easier. They were introduced in the early to mid twentieth century. The first design for an electric stove was patented in 1896. Electric stoves and gas-powered stoves that rely on electricity are used in many homes today.

Heating and Cooling

Electric cooling benefited the people of the early to mid twentieth century in two main ways: air conditioning and refrigeration. Willis Carrier's "Apparatus for Treating Air" was originally envisioned as a way to control humidity in homes and offices, but it was extremely dangerous because it used ammonia to cool down the system. Eventually, Carrier found a safer replacement for ammonia, and air conditioning units found their way into the businesses that needed them most: crowded movie theaters.

Business owners soon saw the benefits of installing air conditioning units in factories. Cool air seemed to make people work better and faster. Buildings were becoming taller because elevators were becoming more common, and air conditioning helped cool the upper floors. Eventually it found its way into homes, especially in the Southern states where heat and humidity often made summers unbearable.

Electric refrigeration came along in the early 1900s because of a need in breweries and the meat packing industry to keep their products cool. By the 1920s, finding an electric refrigerator in the home was commonplace. Today, 99 percent of homes in the United States have at least one refrigerator. Twenty-six percent have more than one.

Before electric heating, people had clever ways of keeping their homes warm. The Romans had fire-burning furnaces and a system of pipes in the walls and floor through which heat could travel throughout the house. The first central heating system was patented by an African American inventor named Alice Parker in 1919. An electric fan was added to push the heat through the home in 1935. Most heaters today burn natural gas for fuel, but are controlled by electric thermostats. These give the homeowner a greater ability to raise and lower the heat as necessary in the winter months.

DID YOU KNOW:

The introduction of air conditioning is why we have summer blockbuster movies today. Air conditioned theaters were places to come and cool off on sweltering days before cooling units became more common in homes.

Electricity and Transportation

During Thomas Jefferson's presidency in the 1800s, he hoped that, one day, explorers would find a waterway that

Electric streetcars first appeared in the United States during the late 1800s. This one could be caught in front of Cincinnati's city hall in 1890.

connected the Atlantic and Pacific Oceans. During this time, ships carried people and goods across the oceans and rivers. A trip across an ocean often took months. The ships relied on wind power to push sails. Travel by sea was dangerous. Food and water supplies often ran low. Travel across the American landscape was not much better. What roads existed could be traveled by horse-drawn wagon, but a journey took a lot of time. In cities, horse-drawn carriages and streetcars provided transportation, but leaving one's neighborhood was more of a chore because of the time it took to arrive and then turn around and travel home. Electricity helped ease the discomfort and inconvenience of travel.

The electric trolley or streetcar was introduced in the 1880s. Over the next few decades, horse-drawn trolleys and other animal-powered vehicles were replaced by electrical cars and trains. With funding and help from his former employer Thomas Edison, a man named Frank

Julian Sprague began to develop electric railway systems in cities across the United States. The first was installed in Richmond, Virginia, in 1887, to enormous success. He eventually sold the company to the Edison General Electric Company and went to work on his next project: improving electric elevators. Today, city dwellers still rely on trolleys and electrically powered subways and trains to get around.

Vehicles next had a massive effect on transportation. One of the first cars was invented in 1769, and was steam powered. The first electric car was introduced in the 1830s by a Scottish inventor named Robert Anderson. New models kept coming, but one fact remained: cars were a luxury item, made one at a time, and unavailable and unaffordable to most people. Then in 1908, Henry Ford introduced the Model T car. It was produced on an assembly line and made cars affordable for more people. In 1912, a Model T could be purchased for around $650 (around $16,165 today). The arrival of the gas-powered car dealt a blow to the electric cars and vehicles of the time. However, electricity still had a role to play. The electric starter was introduced by Charles Kettering in 1912. It made both gas and electrical power necessary for cars to run. This is still the case in most cars today. Electric and hybrid vehicles have become more popular in recent years because of concerns over the expense and pollution created by gas-burning cars. Modern electric vehicles run on rechargeable batteries, while hybrids have both a gas engine and an electric motor. They work together to move the car.

Similar to cars, the majority of airplanes burn fuel but rely heavily on electrically powered systems. Lights inside the plane help keep the flight crew and passengers safe. Outer lights aid in air traffic safety during takeoff, mid-flight, and landing. Modern airplanes rely on computer technology in the cockpit to help pilots take off and land safely, and detect issues with the aircraft. Advances in flight technology have made a trip that used to take months by boat into one that can be completed in hours.

Today, more people want to use electricity as the sole way to power a plane. Designs are still in early stages. However, if issues can be ironed out, electrically powered planes could help reduce pollution and provide less expensive, quieter flights to passengers.

Electricity Improves Communication

Although the electric telegraph was a profoundly important innovation in the mid-nineteenth century, it was soon overshadowed by the telephone. In 1876, Alexander Graham Bell patented his telephone device, and by 1880, there were 47,900 telephones in use in the United States. The telephone dominated the field of communication for the next century. Because of these early innovations that used electricity, technology was able to advance yet again in the late twentieth century and the twenty-first century.

Alexander Graham Bell was asked to demonstrate the telephone's use to Queen Victoria in 1878. This phone was used to answer the queen's call at a nearby cottage.

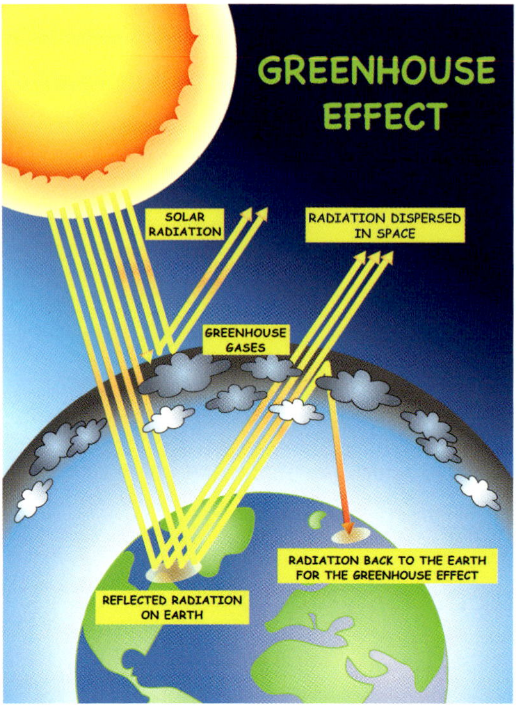

This diagram shows how the greenhouse effect works. More carbon dioxide in the atmosphere means that more solar radiation and heat from the sun is absorbed.

While computer technology started out as steam-powered problem-solving machines in the nineteenth century, they would eventually become the dominant method of communication with the help of electricity. The World Wide Web began in 1989 as a way for scientists to communicate information globally, but by 1993, browsing software became available for everyone to use. Development and marketing of the personal computer during the 1980s and 1990s would lead to handheld communication. Today, many people around the world are connected almost constantly through personal computers and cellular telephone devices, powered by rechargeable batteries.

The Downsides of Electricity Use

Electricity has sparked some of the most important innovations in history. However, its worldwide use has had side effects that are slowly becoming global issues.

Global Warming and Pollution

When fossil fuels are burned, they release carbon dioxide and other pollutants into the atmosphere. There the pollutants absorb sunlight and radiation that once bounced off Earth's surface and ended up in space. With these heat-causing elements trapped in the atmosphere, the planet's average temperature increases. This is called the greenhouse effect. Power plants that burn coal contribute most of the 2 billion tons (1.8 billion metric tons) of carbon dioxide that leads to global warming. While a warmer climate might sound pleasant after a chilly winter, the effects are actually very damaging. As the temperature rises, it melts ice in glaciers, destroying wildlife habitats and causing sea levels to rise. Global warming has also caused a number of extreme weather phenomena, including droughts, hurricanes, and heavy rainfall.

Coal-burning power plants also cause pollution. Harmful gases released by the burning of coal create smog. Smog can cause asthma and damage to the lungs. These same gases also mix with rainfall, leading to acid rain, which can kill plants and fish. Burning coal also releases mercury, which gets into groundwater, affecting fish. Anything that eats those fish, including humans, is in danger of mercury poisoning.

Overuse of Fossil Fuels

Fossil fuels are a finite resource. That means at some point they will run out. Humans use around 12 billion tons (11 billion metric tons) of oil every year in order to fuel cars and run power plants. At this rate, the world will run out of oil by 2052, according to some estimates. Gas and coal would then take over as our main sources of energy, but gas would then run out by 2060. Coal would follow in 2088, leaving behind a lot more pollution. Coal is by far the biggest polluter of the fossil fuels. Work is being done to find and use sustainable and clean sources of energy, but these also have some disadvantages.

Nuclear power is often considered a cleaner resource, since fission doesn't produce carbon dioxide. However, uranium is also finite. Use of nuclear resources creates waste, which is radioactive. It will continue to be radioactive for hundreds of thousands of years and must be handled with extreme care. Nuclear power also carries a potential for accidents. In 1986, a nuclear power plant in Ukraine known as Chernobyl melted down, killing thirty employees and making a larger area uninhabitable. A 2011 tsunami resulted in three nuclear meltdowns in Fukishima, Japan. Disasters like this lead to deaths and disability due to radiation poisoning.

Wind power is a quickly developing source of power in the United States. It relies on wind turbines to create electricity. The method is controversial because of the amount of space required to install wind turbines. Many people see them as ugly. They might ruin the view of a

Offshore oil drilling accounted for 30 percent of oil output in 2015, according to the US Energy Information Administration.

nice field or other landscape. Also, wind is unpredictable. Turbines won't work on a still day.

Hydropower relies on flowing water to get its power. It disrupts aquatic ecosystems, can cause droughts, and dams up valuable water resources like rivers that people rely on for drinking water farther downstream. This is also not always a reliable resource because of drought. If a river dries up, the source of power vanishes along with it.

Use of electricity as a resource is still pretty new when compared to the thousands of years that came before. With time and more technology, perhaps more efficient energy can replace current ways of creating electricity, saving time and the planet.

The Columbia River Gorge in the northwest United States is home to a number of wind farms.

CHAPTER FOUR

Electricity Today and Tomorrow

The twentieth century saw electric power begin and become one of the world's most valuable resources. However, the twenty-first century has continued to build upon the invention by creating new technologies. In addition to all of the new ways that electricity is being produced, people are working on brand-new ways to store energy, make it more efficient, and apply it to society.

Advancements in Producing Electricity

In the past few decades, wind, solar, nuclear, biomass, geothermal, and hydroelectric power have become known as more efficient, less environmentally damaging alternatives to the burning of fossil fuels. However, these do not represent all of the possibilities of environmentally conscious power. Work is being done to improve current technology and develop new ways to produce energy.

Wave Energy

If you've ever swum in the ocean on a windy day or been caught on a boat during a storm, you know the power of waves. Imagine using that power to create energy. There are theories that waves off the coast of the United States have the potential to create 2.64 trillion kilowatt hours of electricity per year. Almost 4 trillion total kilowatt hours of electricity were consumed in the United States in 2017, so wave energy has the potential to provide around 66 percent of America's necessary power.

The study of wave energy is not new. A Parisian named Girard filed a patent in 1799 for a machine he had built with his son to harness the energy of ocean waves. They wanted to find a way to help run pumps and sawmills. In the 1940s, a former Japanese naval commander named Yoshio Masuda created hundreds of navigation buoys with lights that ran on wave energy. In 1973, an oil crisis had governments all over the world searching for alternatives to fossil fuel energy. Prototypes, or examples, of devices for capturing wave energy were created in the following years. One of these was called the Edinburgh Duck. It could take wave power and convert it into energy. However, wave energy was a long way from becoming a popular power source.

Wave energy can be captured in a few different ways. One method involves channeling waves into narrower spaces in order to maximize the wave's power as it spins a

DID YOU KNOW:

One of the biggest issues preventing the development of wave energy is water itself. Salt water corrodes, or weakens, metal. Metal components would need to be replaced often as they break down. Repairs would be costly.

turbine. Another channels the water into a reservoir where it is sent through a turbine at a lower elevation. As the turbine spins, in both methods, energy is the by-product.

Building a Better Wind Turbine

Off the coast of Scotland in the North Sea lies the world's first floating wind farm, called the Hywind project. The five turbines that make up this wind farm are about 830 feet (253 m) in height, but 256 feet (78 m) of this lies below the ocean's surface. Enormous suction anchors—three per turbine—hold the turbine in place so it doesn't drift, and 111 tons of weight (101 metric tons) per anchor keep the turbine upright. This allows for turbines to be placed in deeper water since they don't need to be fastened directly to the ground. Out on open water, there are fewer complaints about the noise the turbines make, and they no longer take up valuable land space. The five turbines that make up the Hywind project have the potential to power twenty thousand homes. Non-floating offshore wind turbine farms are in production along the East Coast of the United States as well. The plan is to have them up and running by 2021.

Hywind Scotland officially opened on October 18, 2017. From underwater anchor to the top of the highest blade, one of these turbines is three times as tall as the Statue of Liberty.

In 2014, Altaeros Energies, an MIT startup company, introduced the Buoyant Airborne Turbine (BAT). It hovers high above the earth to capture powerful wind currents that can't be reached by regular turbines. Carried by a large helium-filled structure up to 2,000 feet (600 m) into the air, the BAT can generate twice the energy of its ground-based counterparts. In the past, the turbine has been tethered over Anchorage, Alaska, a region that is difficult to provide with power. Fuel there is expensive to ship because roads are not reliable year round, solar power isn't reliable because the sun doesn't shine well enough, and anchoring ground-based wind turbines isn't possible in the permafrost of Alaska.

Ground-based turbines are also getting bigger. Blades and rotors are growing in size to produce more energy. Turbines are also getting taller to catch more powerful wind currents. The seventeen turbines that make up the

Hancock Wind Project in Hancock County, Maine, stand about 574 feet (175 m) in height. The average wind turbine stands at about 466 feet (142 m). Soon, though, turbines will be nearly twice that tall. When completed in 2021, a turbine called the Haliade-X, financed by General Electric, will stand at 853 feet (260 m). Each of the blades of this turbine will measure 351 feet (107 m) in length.

Improvements to Solar Energy

The idea of solar power has been around for centuries. First, in 1839, a French physicist named Edmond Becquerel discovered that the sun produced energy that could be stored. This is called a photovoltaic effect. A few decades later, in 1876, Kings College professor William Grylls Adams and his student, Richard Day, exposed the element selenium to light and discovered that this

Many people don't like the look of solar panels on the roof of their home, but technology is in progress that will make the solar panel a more appealing element of home design.

produced electricity. The silicon solar cell was introduced in the 1950s, but it was very expensive. Since 2009, the price of solar energy has gone down 70 percent, making adopting solar power a much more affordable option for homes and businesses.

Two main technologies that drive solar power are photovoltaics and concentrated solar power. Photovoltaics generate energy directly from the sun. This is done when light from the sun hits a solar panel. A direct current is created in the panel. Electricity is produced and converted into electricity that can be used in the home or an office. Concentrated solar power devices use mirrors to reflect sunlight onto receivers that collect heat and use it to make energy.

Today, there is a lot being done to make solar power more attractive and affordable. Different ingredients are being used on panels to lower their cost. Some of the ingredients currently being used to make solar panels are very dangerous. New ingredients not only help lower cost but also help protect people making and installing the panels. Likewise, solar panels aren't that nice to look at. Many homeowners complain that solar panels make their homes look unattractive. However, a company called Sistine Solar is creating custom solar panels that double as art or blend seamlessly into the existing color and texture of a house's roof. Other steps are being taken to make sure solar power is more popular in places with a lot of sunshine. In California, new homes are required to have solar panels. Using solar panels also helps promote renewable energy.

Other structures are using solar technology. One example is solar-powered roads. Certain roadways and sidewalks in the United States and China are being laid with photovoltaic technology that converts energy from the sun. This is in the early testing stages and is extremely expensive, but not only do these solar panels create clean energy, they could be used to melt snow and ice from roadways in the winter months.

Solar power is also becoming a topic in fashion. At the University of Tokyo and the RIKEN research institute in Japan, researchers are working to develop small, flexible, lightweight, and water-resistant solar panels that can be sewn into fabric. This technology could make it so that people no longer have to charge cell phones or other devices at a power outlet. They could simply draw power from the clothing they wear.

New Ways to Store Electricity

Batteries have come a long way since the eras of the Baghdad batteries and the voltaic pile. The Eveready battery was introduced in 1898. It powered another new invention, the flashlight. As technology has changed over the past century, batteries have changed as well.

There are two main types of batteries: primary batteries and rechargeable batteries. Primary batteries wear out over time and cannot be revived. They are usually used in remote controls and some toys. Rechargeable batteries can be placed in a recharging unit that is plugged in to an electrical outlet. There they can charge to full strength and be used again.

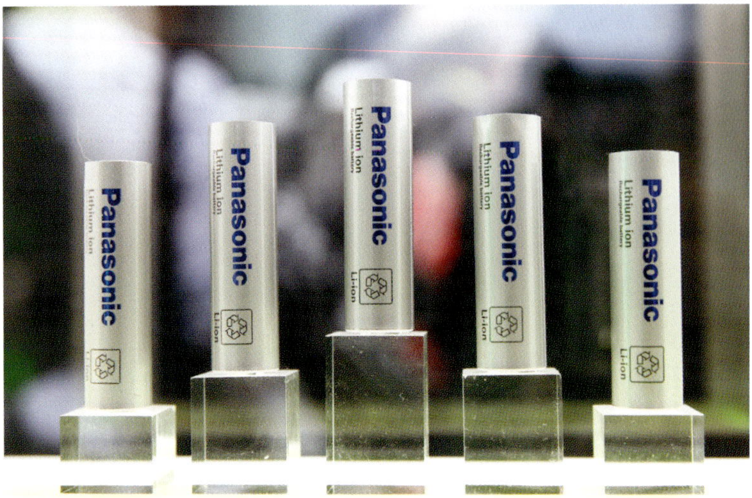

Lithium-ion rechargeable batteries have made smartphones and tablets possible, but new battery technology is always in the works.

New battery technology means finding ways to make batteries that can hold a charge better and for a longer period of time. Lithium-ion batteries are the most commonly used batteries in today's smartphones and iPads. However, they have a number of flaws. They can overheat and explode easily. They also break down over time. Researchers are working to find technology to replace lithium-ion batteries.

Microsupercapacitors

Devices called microsupercapacitors might replace the battery altogether. They have the power of a battery but are stored in a microchip. This technology is quite new. However, if developed more, it would allow devices to grow smaller and no longer need a battery to work.

GLUCOSE POWER

The human body converts sugar, called glucose, into energy. What if you could power an electronic device in a similar manner? The answer lies in bio-batteries.

Bio-batteries have been in development by Sony since 2001. Prototypes of this device use enzymes to help break down plant-based matter. This can generate enough to run an mp3 player. In other words, waste paper or any paper product could be recycled into energy. However, any kind of sugar could be used to power these devices. One 2007 demonstration even showed the battery drawing power from a sports drink. Bio-batteries could even one day be powered by the bacteria found in human sweat.

Researchers at Binghamton University in New York City created a flexible battery in 2017. The substance is so fabric-like that it could be used to fashion socks or other athletic wear, blood sugar sensors for diabetic wearers, heart sensors, or even wearable gear for the military.

This Sony employee demonstrates how the bio-battery works in 2011. The glucose in the cardboard is converted into energy.

Here, Panasonic CEO Joseph Taylor demonstrates the flexibility of a new type of lithium-ion battery.

Microsupercapacitors can also be charged much faster than batteries. New technology is even allowing for a thousand microsupercapacitors to be manufactured in a minute. Being able to quickly make them means the price of these devices goes down. This means that people might be able to use the microsupercapacitors more often in the future.

Foam and Flexible Batteries

The Jenax J.Flex battery is a paper-like device that can be folded, bent, or even rolled up without causing damage. It's also waterproof, which means that it can be put into clothing, watches, belts, or other accessories.

Foam batteries do away with the flammable acid contained inside batteries, replacing it with a porous foam copper-based substance. This substance is light and helps batteries to last longer.

Two hundred years ago, the idea of homes and businesses powered by electricity was the stuff of science fiction. Today, we can't imagine life without it. Imagine the technology that will be created over the next two hundred years!

GLOSSARY

alternating current A type of power that reverses direction and can travel faster and farther and at a higher voltage than a direct current.

amber effect An early name for static electricity, created when a piece of fossilized amber was rubbed against another material and gained a power of attraction.

assembly line A factory method in which items move from one workstation to the next. Each worker adds an element to the larger piece being built.

bio-battery A device in which enzymes are used to break down natural sugars, creating energy.

biomass Organic materials from plants and animals that can create power when burned.

converter A device through which an electric current is channeled that changes its voltage or currency, or from alternating current to direct current or vice versa.

direct current A flow of electricity that travels in only one direction.

electron A subatomic particle contained in every atom; it carries a negative charge.

enzyme A protein in the body that is used to start biochemical reactions.

Faraday wheel An electric generator in which a disc or cylinder spins near a magnetic field, creating energy.

filament A metal wire in lightbulbs that helps conduct electricity.

fission The act of splitting an atom, which results in production of energy.

fossil fuel Fuels, such as gas, coal, and petroleum, made from once-living organisms.

geothermal energy Power created using the earth's natural heat.

hypothesis An early theory that is based on limited information and requires further study and experimentation for proof.

incandescent lightbulb A bulb that creates light when a wire filament is heated to a high temperature and begins to glow.

Leyden jar A device used to store electricity.

lightning rod A metal structure mounted on a building that diverts the energy from a lightning strike into the ground, keeping the building safe.

patent An official license of ownership of an invention.

telegraph A device for sending messages across an electrical wire.

transformer A device that is used to raise or lower the voltage of an alternating current in order for it to be used and transported safely.

turbine A machine that is made to spin by water, wind, steam, or another force, generating electrical power.

voltaic pile A battery formed from metal discs layered with pieces of saltwater-soaked cloth.

FURTHER INFORMATION

Books

Bakke, Gretchen. *The Grid: The Fraying Wires Between Americans and Our Energy Future*. New York: Bloomsbury, 2017.

Brown, Lester R. *The Great Transition: Shifting from Fossil Fuels to Solar and Wind Energy*. New York: W.W. Norton and Company, 2015.

Cawthorne, Nigel. *Tesla vs Edison: The Life-Long Feud That Electrified the World*. New York: Chartwell Books, 2016.

Green, Dan. *DK Eyewitness Books: Energy*. New York: DK, 2016.

Peake, Stephen. *Renewable Energy: Power for a Sustainable Future*. New York: Oxford University Press, 2018.

Websites

Department of Energy

https://www.energy.gov/science-innovation/clean-energy

The US Department of Energy shares a comprehensive guide to current environmentally friendly technology in the United States.

How to Make a Volta Pile

http://www.instructables.com/id/How-to-make-a-volta-pile

This guide offers simple instructions on constructing your own voltaic pile.

The Thomas Edison Center at Menlo Park

http://www.menloparkmuseum.org

This historical museum center allows visitors to walk through Edison's laboratories at Menlo Park.

Videos

Biography: Thomas Edison

https://www.youtube.com/watch?v=HQ2RJC1a8T0

This short biography explores the life and inventions of Thomas Edison.

How I Harnessed the Wind

https://www.ted.com/talks/william_kamkwamba_how_i_harnessed_the_wind

Listen to William Kamkwamba, a Malawian boy who built his own windmill at the age of fourteen, speak about his work with harnessing the wind.

SELECTED BIBLIOGRAPHY

Atkinson, Nancy. "Who Discovered Electricity?" Universe Today. March 3, 2014. https://www.universetoday.com/82402/who-discovered-electricity.

BBC News. "Riddle of 'Baghdad's Batteries.'" BBC News. February 27, 2003. http://news.bbc.co.uk/2/hi/science/nature/2804257.stm.

Bellis, Mary. "Biography of Luigi Galvani." ThoughtCo. January 24, 2018. https://www.thoughtco.com/luigi-galvani-theory-animal-electricity-1991692.

———. "History of the Automobile: The Assembly Line." ThoughtCo. February 27, 2018. https://www.thoughtco.com/history-of-car-assembly-line-4072559.

———. "The History of the Electric Telegraph and Telegraphy." ThoughtCo. August 7, 2017. https://www.thoughtco.com/the-history-of-the-electric-telegraph-and-telegraphy-1992542.

Deffree, Suzanne. "Faraday Discovers Electromagnetic Induction, August 29, 1831." EDN Network. August 29, 2017. https://www.edn.com/electronics-blogs/edn-moments/4394972/Faraday-discovers-electromagnetic-induction--August-29--1831.

Franklin Institute. "Benjamin Franklin and the Kite Experiment." https://www.fi.edu/benjamin-franklin/kite-key-experiment.

Gibbens, Sarah. "See the World's First Floating Wind Farm." National Geographic. October 18, 2017. https://news.nationalgeographic.com/2017/10/wind-farm-renewable-energy-scotland-video-spd.

Gunderman, Richard. "The Extraordinary Life of Nikola Tesla." Smithsonian.com. January 5, 2018. https://www.smithsonianmag.com/innovation/extraordinary-life-nikola-tesla-180967758.

Jones, LuAnn. "Electricity's Impact on Rural Life." NCPedia. 1985. https://www.ncpedia.org/agriculture/electricity.

Jonnes, Jill. *Empires of Light: Edison, Tesla, Westinghouse, and the Race to Electrify the World.* New York: Random House, 2004.

Lindeman, Todd. "1.3 Billion Are Living in the Dark." *Washington Post.* November 6, 2015. https://www.washingtonpost.com/graphics/world/world-without-power.

Matulka, Rebecca. "The History of the Electric Car." Energy.gov. September 15, 2014. https://www.energy.gov/articles/history-electric-car.

MIT Libraries Special Collections. "The Voltaic Pile." https://libraries.mit.edu/collections/vail-collection/topics/electricity/the-voltaic-pile.

ReEnergy Holdings LLC. "What Is Biomass?" ReEnergy Holdings LLC. https://www.reenergyholdings.com/renewable-energy/what-is-biomass.

Rinkesh. "What Is Wave Energy?" Conserve Energy Future. https://www.conserve-energy-future.com/waveenergy.php.

Ross, Rachel. "Who Invented the Refrigerator?" LiveScience. February 8, 2017. https://www.livescience.com/57797-refrigerator-history.html.

Semigran, Rachel. "The True Story Behind Ben Franklin's Lightning Experiment." Mental Floss. August 10, 2015. http://mentalfloss.com/article/66551/true-story-behind-ben-franklins-lightning-experiment.

Siegel, RP. "Wind Power: Pros and Cons." Triple Pundit. June 27, 2012. https://www.triplepundit.com/special/energy-options-pros-and-cons/wind-power-pros-cons.

Sony. "Sony Develops 'Bio Battery' Generating Electricity from Sugar." Sony. August 23, 2007. https://www.sony.net/SonyInfo/News/Press/200708/07-074E/index.html.

Waxman, Olivia B. "The Real Reason Why Daylight Saving Time Is a Thing." TIME. November 1, 2017. http://time.com/4549397/daylight-saving-time-history-politics.

INDEX

Page numbers in **boldface** are illustrations.

ABOUT THE AUTHOR

Bethany Bryan's interest in electricity was sparked by early experiments involving Wint-O-Green Life Savers. She is the author of multiple books, and especially loves writing about historical feuds. She lives in Kansas City, Missouri, home of Kansas City Power & Light Company, founded by Edwin R. Weeks in 1882 after he attended an expo in Philadelphia and was inspired by an electric arc light demonstration he saw there.